Talking about Jesus

Talking about Jesus

Discovering the Joy of Sharing Jesus' Story

DAVID M. STRATTON

RESOURCE *Publications* · Eugene, Oregon

TALKING ABOUT JESUS
Discovering the Joy of Sharing Jesus' Story

Resource Publications
An Imprint of Wipf and Stock Publishers
199 W. 8th Ave., Suite 3
Eugene, OR 97401

www.wipfandstock.com

PAPERBACK ISBN: 978-1-5326-7539-3
HARDCOVER ISBN: 978-1-5326-7540-9
EBOOK ISBN: 978-1-5326-7541-6

Manufactured in the U.S.A.   03/06/19

Dedicated to all those with a passion for sharing Jesus' story
and to all those seeking to nurture such a passion.

"The seventy returned with joy . . ." (Luke 10:17a, NRSV)

Contents

Introduction

Iwas afraid to dive off the high board at Holliday Lake. When I was an adolescent, three mothers who were friends, one of whom was my mother, took their children to Holliday Lake State Park in Appomattox County, Virginia every Friday during the summer. In the deep water at Holliday Lake, there was a platform with two diving boards on opposing ends. One of those diving boards was much higher than the other.

I was a good swimmer and loved the water. I dove off the low board many times, but the high board scared me. I'm not sure why. Then one day my best friend, Frankie, asked me why I never dove off the high board. Reluctantly I confided with him my fear.

Frankie was very understanding. He gave me a few pointers and coaxed me up the ladder to the high board. He dove first. I might have chickened out and climbed back down the ladder but, at that point, I was more afraid of being teased by the other kids in line behind me than I was of diving off the high board.

So, off I went. I nailed the dive perfectly and it was an exhilarating experience! I asked myself why I waited so long and I had no good answer. From then on I almost always dove off the high board rather than the low board. But for a long time, because of my fear, I missed out on an experience that brought me much joy.

I think most Christians of this culture are in a similar situation about something much more important and joy-producing than recreational swimming. There's an act essential to the identity of followers of Christ that is designed to delight our hearts and the hearts of others. It's also an act that strikes fear in the hearts of many Christians: talking to others about Jesus.

Wait! Don't stop reading yet! I'm serious when I say talking about Jesus is designed to be a joy-producing experience. Sure, talking about Jesus can change our world in wonderful ways. Yes, Jesus did command his followers to talk with others about him. These are really good reasons to talk with others about Jesus. But there's also substantial New Testament evidence that talking to others about Jesus often brings joy to the one doing the talking.

In Luke 10, Jesus appointed 70 people that he sent out to be his missionaries. Before he sent them, in addition to giving some instructions, he was blunt in warning them that their mission had the potential to be dangerous. When the 70 returned, we are specifically told that they were filled with joy and Jesus himself was positively giddy as they told him of their experiences (Luke 10:17–18).

On the wild day when the Holy Spirit came at Pentecost and filled all believers, Peter preached a great sermon about Jesus but we're also told that all Christ-followers declared God's deeds of power (Acts 2:11). The result was about 3,000 people becoming followers of Jesus (Acts 2:41). These believers, new and old, got together regularly and had *glad hearts* (Acts 2:46). Joy is linked to talking about Jesus and the resulting fellowship

To be sure, there are New Testament examples of believers getting into serious trouble for talking about Jesus and that still happens today. But we should remember that Jesus encouraged his followers to leap for joy when they are treated harshly on account of him (Luke 6:22–23). If we trust Christ, then there's reason for joy even when things don't exactly go smoothly in our efforts to talk about him. Sounds weird, I know. But the cross opened the door to the ultimate joy of the resurrection so, when it comes to Jesus, we shouldn't be surprised at ironic paths to joy.

What's true on the pages of the New Testament has also been true in my personal experience. When I have opportunities to talk about Jesus with those who have not yet decided to follow him, even if those moments don't result in an immediate profession of faith, I experience great joy. So I'd like to play the role of Frankie in this little book. I want to help believers to overcome a fear that prevents a great experience of joy. In order to be Frankie-like, I need to be understanding of the fears that prevent Christians from talking about Jesus. The first way I'd like to be sympathetic is to assure you that I'm not going to try to force you to talk about Jesus in a particular way that is often not very helpful and sometimes damaging

A well-meaning way that evangelicals have talked about Jesus in the recent past and sometimes still today involves a "sales pitch" type approach summarized in tracts like The Romans Road, Steps to Peace with God, The Four Spiritual Laws and others. My earliest training in talking about Jesus utilized this method. Frankly, I was never very comfortable with this high pressure technique that reduces the gospel to a few bullet points. In my experience, most Christians who are taught this way of talking about Jesus don't stick with it (which may explain why we're in decades-long decline in evangelical effectiveness in evangelism) and then they feel guilty because they think this is the way that they're supposed to be talking about Jesus.

I'm not trying to be overly negative about the "sales pitch" approach of talking about Jesus. Those who developed it were devout Christians and this method has certainly done some good. But I think most Christians are extremely uncomfortable with this approach and, thankfully, the "sales pitch" method is not the only method of talking about Jesus.

So if I'm not going to give you the "sales pitch" method, what am I going to do to increase your comfort level and thereby your joy in talking about Jesus? I'm going to take some major elements of Jesus' story—his birth, his life, his death, his resurrection, his ongoing presence, and his return—and briefly flesh out one big idea about each of these elements. Just one. Why do I think this will help?

For a long time, evangelicals have emphasized the importance of sharing one's personal testimony as a way of sharing Christ. I agree this is important. We need to be ready to share the impact

Christ has made on our lives, how he has clarified our direction in life, and challenged us in healthy ways—how he has saved us. Such testimony reveals our passion about Christ and we're more apt to gain a hearing concerning that for which we're passionate.

But at some point we must move beyond saying Jesus means a lot to us and get to Jesus' story. This is crucial. The Apostle Paul called the gospel, the story of Jesus, "the power of God" (Romans 1:16, NRSV). As we share the story of Jesus we share the power of God and the power of God can accomplish a lot when it's shared.

I'm not saying that we should share the entire story of Jesus in every opportunity that we have to be his witnesses. I don't expect for you to memorize the entire story of Jesus and be ready to regurgitate it. But what if you could remember just one big idea from each major element of Jesus' story? Might the Spirit help you to color in, to expand on that big idea when doors open to be witnesses for Jesus? This is my prayer.

What follows is not a systematic Christology. Any trained theologian reading what I write on the various elements of Jesus' life might well scream at me about leaving out this, that or another thing or about emphasizing this when I should have emphasized that. But I'm not trying to tell you everything about Jesus' story. I just want to give you a brief, easy-to-remember framework that may help you in talking to others about Jesus when you get the chance or make the chance.

I'm not trying to reduce Jesus to a few bullet points. The Apostle Paul wrote that the riches of Christ are boundless (Ephesians 3:8). I don't mean to imply that the handful of big ideas about Jesus on the pages that follow exhaust the immeasurable riches of Christ. I do hope these brief glimpses at Christ may be good starting points that help you to gain confidence in sharing the riches of Christ with others.

My big ideas about these elements of Jesus' story are, no doubt, colored by the times and the culture in which I live. If I lived in another time or in another culture, I might have decided that a different set of big ideas is more important in sharing Christ. The big ideas that I settled on from the elements of Jesus' life that I have chosen are the product of decades of studying Jesus' life and trying to proclaim his good news to others in a way that will be persuasive.

Because I think brevity is important to making this resource helpful I make the assumption that those reading this very little book are fairly well acquainted with the story of Jesus. I don't go into any detail in telling the story of each of the elements of Jesus' life that I have chosen. Instead I assume that you are somewhat conversant with the story. I simply want to give you a big idea that might help you to share why that element makes Jesus worth following.

In 1 Corinthians 1:23 the Apostle Paul wrote to believers, ". . . we proclaim Christ . . ." (NRSV). That's another way of saying, "We talk about Jesus." I hope what follows helps us to be more comfortable doing just that for his glory.

1

His Birth

The big idea: Jesus' birth shows us that lowliness is next to godliness.

One of my favorite Christmas stories didn't begin as a Christmas story but as a tale written by the Brothers Grimm, "The Fisherman and His Wife." The couple lived in a filthy shack. One day, the fisherman caught only one fish, but it was a special flounder. The flounder explained it really was an enchanted prince and asked to be placed back in the ocean. The fisherman complied. He returned home and told his wife about the fish, initiating a cycle of unbridled greed.

The wife told the fisherman he should have asked for something and she sent him back to ask for a cottage. The fisherman didn't want to go, but his wife was insistent, so he did her bidding. The flounder asked what the wife wanted, and the fisherman described her desire for a cottage. The flounder told the fisherman to go home; his wife already had the cottage she requested. The fisherman returned to a new cottage and suggested his wife should be happy now, but she wasn't.

Soon she sent her husband back to ask for a stone mansion. Next, she wanted to be king. After this, she insisted on becoming emperor, then pope. The flounder kept granting the wife's greedy wishes, and her power and prestige multiplied.

Then she sent her husband to tell the flounder to make her like God. Quaking with fear, the fisherman did as he was told. After he made the request, the flounder told the fisherman to go back home, where he would find his wife in the filthy shack, just as she began. The story ends by stating the couple dwells in that shack to this very day.

Many interpret the step back to the shack as a punishment upon the wife's greed. I disagree. The flounder merely gave the wife what she sought.

The willful wife wanted to be like God. So the fish took her from a position of glory to a dirty shack—sort of like how Jesus left the glory of heaven for a dirty stable in Bethlehem.

This is perhaps the most shocking and wonderful thing about Jesus' birth. It's shocking enough that God became flesh and dwelt with humans at all. But as long as God was going to take this stunning step, we would expect God to at least assume a more God-like station among humans. Instead, God became flesh in the lowliest, most scandalous circumstances possible.

Rather than being born to a king and queen in a castle, wrapped in a royal blanket and laid in a golden crib, Jesus was born to a poor, unmarried peasant couple in a stable, wrapped in rags, and laid in a feed trough. This was no accident on God's part. As the Apostle Paul wrote: "God chose what is weak in the world to shame the strong; God chose what is low and despised in the world, things that are not, to reduce to nothing things that are, so that no one might boast in the presence of God" (1 Corinthians 1:27–29, NRSV).

God's ambition, if you will, in entering the world was not for prestige to our thinking. The fisherman's wife was closer to God's revelation of God's self in this world when she was in the shack than when she held positions of power and glory. The story of the fisherman and his wife and the story of Jesus' birth show us that becoming like God in this world has nothing to do with worldly notions of glory. The birth of Christ shows that lowliness is next to godliness.

I'm not saying we should all move out of our houses, apartments or other comfy dwellings in order to live in filthy shacks. I am saying that Jesus, even before he could speak, advocated radically different aspirations for life than the pursuits that typically enamor humanity. From the day he was born, Jesus showed us that what God considers most important is different from what humans normally consider most important.

Over the years there has been lots of discussion surrounding the Virgin Birth and the nature of the incarnation and rightly so. The birth narratives of Matthew and Luke reveal the miraculous conception of Jesus, attributing it to the Holy Spirit. With his birth, Jesus was the incarnation of God—in his life the life and power of God were in action. These are wonderful mysteries pointing to Jesus' identity as the Son of God—mysteries worth marveling over and cherishing.

But connected to the breathtaking realities of the Virgin Birth and incarnation is something revolutionary revealed in humble birth of Jesus. With his birth Christ began turning the popular values of our culture upside down. He reduces to nothing the ambitions that consume us. As the Apostle Paul put it, "For you know the generous act of our Lord Jesus Christ, that though he was rich, yet for your sakes he became poor, so that by his poverty you might become rich" (2 Cor. 8:9, NRSV). The cry of a newborn baby wrapped in rags in a feed trough in a stable in Bethlehem declared that lowliness is next to godliness.

Questions to ponder

- How might you use Jesus' birth to talk about Jesus?
- How might the Advent/Christmas season provide openings to talk about Jesus?

- In what ways might the birth of Jesus give us an opening to talk about the emptiness of the standard consumeristic and power-hungry ambitions our culture?

Just one conversation idea among many

Friend: [In December] The Christmas season is so impossibly busy. On top of everything else there are all the parties and family gatherings. There all the decorations to put up and all the presents to buy. I'm run ragged and my credit cards are maxed out.

Christian: You're right. The really sad thing is that the typical Christmas practices of our culture absolutely turn upside down the values God revealed in Christ at his birth. Through Jesus, God became flesh among humans. God could have done that in any way God wanted. God could have had Jesus born in the most prestigious, most comfortable royal circumstances. Instead, God chose the lowliest and most scandalous setting possible for the birth of the Savior. He was born to a poor, unmarried peasant couple, wrapped in rags and laid in a feed trough in a dirty stable. Jesus' birth shows us that lowliness is next to godliness and exposes the emptiness of our standard ambitions and offers the hope of another away—a better way . . .

2

His Life

The big idea: Jesus' life shows us that God insists on treating us much better than we deserve and that God expects us to do the same toward others.

What, if any, belief is unique to the Christian faith? What, if anything, differentiates Christianity from other world religions? During a British conference on comparative religions, experts from around the world debated this topic.

They started eliminating possibilities. The incarnation was tossed out because other religions have different versions of gods appearing in human form. The resurrection was cast aside because other religions have accounts of return from death. The debate went on for quite a while with no resolution until C. S. Lewis, a famous Christian author, wandered into the room.

"What's the rumpus about?" Lewis asked, and he was told that his colleagues were discussing Christianity's distinctive contribution among world religions. Lewis responded, "Oh, that's easy. It's grace."

After further discussion the experts agreed with Lewis' quick conclusion. That God's love comes to humans utterly free of charge seems to cut against human instincts and the beliefs of other major religions. Buddhists have the eight-fold path, Hindus emphasize *karma*, Jews prize the covenant, and Muslims have their code of law. In each case there's a way to earn approval. Only Christianity dares to proclaim that God's love comes with no strings attached.[1] God's revolutionary path of grace is revealed in its purest sense in and through Christ. Since God's grace in Christ is what sets Christianity apart then certainly it must be central to talking about Jesus.

It doesn't do us much good to identify grace as the distinctive mark of Christianity unless we're clear about what grace is. Many have heard grace defined accurately as unmerited favor. Yet I prefer to think in terms of the Contemporary English Version's rendering of the Greek word typically translated grace: "God treats us much better than we deserve."[2] To be sure, this phrase seems like an understatement in describing the grace revealed through the life of Christ. Consider these teachings of Jesus:

> Then Peter came to Jesus and asked, 'Lord, how many times shall I forgive my brother or sister who sins against me? Up to seven times?'
> Jesus answered, 'I tell you, not seven times, but seventy-seven times.' (Matthew 18:21–22, NRSV)

> Lend, expecting nothing in return. (Luke 6:35, NRSV)

> Sell your possessions and give to the poor. (Luke 12:33, NIV)

> Do not resist an evildoer. But if anyone strikes you on the right cheek, turn the other also . . . (Matthew 5:39, NRSV)

Clearly these injunctions from Jesus, and others like them, indicate that God in Christ is insistent on treating others better than they deserve and God expects for us to do the same. But, of course, the pinnacle teaching from Christ that reveals his intent to start a revolution of grace is this one: "Love your enemies"

---

1. Yancey, *What's so Amazing about Grace?*, 45
2. See, for example, Romans 3:24 in the Contemporary English Version.

(Matthew 5:44, NRSV). By definition our enemies don't deserve our love, yet this is precisely what Jesus commands. Furthermore, Jesus practiced what he preached concerning the proper response to one's enemies as we'll see later.

Besides his teaching, Jesus' behavior toward others reveals God's heart for treating humans better than they deserve. The law said that a woman brought before him who had been caught in adultery deserved death, but Jesus refused to condemn her and he discouraged others from doing so (John 8:2–11). A hated Samaritan woman who had been through five husbands he empowered to be his missionary (John 4:4–42).[3] He gratefully accepted an anointing from a prostitute and praised her faith (Luke 7:36–50). He touched a leper (Mark 1:40–42). He called a despised tax collector to be one of his disciples and invited himself to dinner with another tax collector to the shock of those around him (Mark 2:14; Luke 19:1–9). He fed multitudes of hungry people without checking first to see if they 'deserved' free food (Mark 6:34–44; 8:1–9). He was called a friend of immoral people and attacked for forming close associations with infamous sinners (Matthew 11:19; Luke 7:34, Luke 15:1–2).

3. Lynn Cohick's research reveals that the Samaritan woman at the well may not have been the immoral outcast many scholars and preachers have depicted her to be. In an age of shorter lifespans, we have no way of knowing how many of her marriages ended with the death of her husband or divorce. If any of her marriages ended in divorce, it is very unlikely that the woman would have initiated divorce proceedings in that culture. Furthermore, in that society there were numerous legal cohabitation arrangements that would not have been considered objectionable and were regularly an economic necessity for women. Many preachers have said the time of day that the woman drew water indicates that she was shunned by society because of her lifestyle but there is no evidence to suggest that the upright women drew water at one time of day and the degenerate women at another. If the woman had moral failings, there is no doubt that Jesus would have been gracious toward her. However, the Samaritan woman may well have been one who suffered much rejection and grief rather than a despised person of low moral fiber. Even so, Jesus' decision to share a cup with a hated Samaritan, to speak with a woman in that setting in that time, and to commission a woman as a missionary is a remarkable display of grace. (Cohick, *Women in the World of the Earliest Christians*, 119–125.)

Jesus' life shows us that God insists on treating humans much better than we deserve and that God expects us to do the same toward others.

I got into a conversation with a young atheist at a wedding reception some years back. We had talked before and he knows I'm a pastor. This is a very sharp, articulate young man. He's also compassionate toward those in need. He started a community garden in the city where he lives to help the needy. At some point he said to me, and I'm paraphrasing slightly, "The basic message of the Bible is 'Don't be a jerk and be kind to others.' I don't need the Bible, or God for that matter, to know this is the way I should live."

I acknowledged that the Bible includes the message he mentioned. Then I went on to say something along these lines: "But when we get to Jesus, he takes it to a whole different level. He said that we should forgive those who do us wrong no matter how many times they do us wrong. He said, when someone strikes you on one cheek, don't hit back; turn the other cheek. He said that we must love our enemies. That goes well beyond simply 'Don't be a jerk and be kind to others.'"

For the first time in the conversation, this articulate young man was left fumbling for something to say and he quickly changed the subject. But I wouldn't let him of the hook that easily. I circled back, asking if he agreed that the teaching of Christ went beyond his summary of the biblical message. He did agree and he said, essentially, those teachings of Christ are crazy.

But his whole demeanor had changed and I could see that the wheels were turning. It was a breakthrough moment. A brief list of teachings outlining Jesus' revolution of grace shattered perhaps his main argument against Christianity—an argument he felt confident in putting before a pastor. He didn't make a profession of faith at that wedding reception, but Jesus' revolutionary teachings about treating others better than they deserve had upset his world in a good way. In my experience, the revolution of grace exemplified in Jesus' life always has this effect when it is shared with others in a healthy way.

Questions to ponder

- How might you use the grace revealed in the life of Christ as the unique contribution of Christianity among world religions to talk about Jesus?

- How might you use a reminder of the latest negative press related to Christianity to talk about God's grace revealed in Christ?

- How might you, in moments of conflict, model the notion that Jesus' life shows us that God insists on treating us much better than we deserve and that God expects us to do the same toward others?

Just one conversation idea among many

Friend: [In a restaurant] That waitress is terrible. She's rude and incompetent. I've been trying to get a refill of tea for 20 minutes! She's not getting a tip from me!

Christian: I don't blame you. Her service has been really bad. I don't want to tip her either. But you know I'm a Christian and Jesus' life and teaching shows us that God is insistent on treating others better than they deserve and he expects us to do the same. Let's show her a little grace. Maybe she's just having a bad day—we've all had them . . .

3

His Death

The big idea: Jesus' death shows us what love is.

If you ask church goers of our culture why Jesus died on the cross, the answer you're likely get is, "To save us from our sins."[1] This is the prevailing "bumper sticker" understanding of the rationale for Jesus' death in churches of this society. Certainly it's true that Jesus' voluntary sacrifice on the cross is all about salvation from sinfulness. After all, the Apostle Paul wrote, ". . . Christ died for our sins in accordance with the scriptures . . ." (1 Corinthians 15:3, NRSV).

It should be noted that forgiveness of sins includes the ways we've violated a Bible-based moral code, but it's much more than this. Fundamentally, sin is about a distortion of our true identity and purpose. Jesus, through the cross, restores our true sense of who we are and what we're supposed to be doing with our lives

---

1. N. T. Wright wisely points out that scriptural references to Jesus' death accomplishing the forgiveness of sins are referring to something much bigger than the forgiveness of the sins of individuals, although this is certainly included. The forgiveness that Jesus wrought through the cross is linked to God's project of global restoration. Jesus brings forgiveness "in both the focused personal sense and the national and cosmic sense." (Wright, *The Day the Revolution Began*, 106.)

now. This is the main thing we should hear in the phrase "forgiveness of sins."[2]

Yet it's important to note that New Testament writers regularly link the forgiveness of sins Jesus achieves through the cross to love. God proves his love for us in that, while we were sinners, Christ died for us (Rom. 5:8). This is love, not that we loved God but that he loved us and sent his Son to be the atoning sacrifice for our sins (1 John 4:10). Jesus loves us and freed us from our sins by his blood (Rev. 1:5). These and other passages show us that Jesus died to forgive our sins and this is an act of love from beginning to end.

Actually we could add to the popular bumper sticker phrase of the reason for Jesus' death with another popular saying along these lines: Jesus died to save us from our sins so we can go to heaven when we die. It's true and more than wonderful that Jesus' death accomplishes forgiveness of sins and opens the doors to a glorious 'heavenly' future for those who trust him. Yet the promise of this glorious future is more closely linked to another part of Jesus' story that we'll consider later, namely his resurrection. In a sense Jesus' death and resurrection are inseparable events—one cannot be fully understood without the other. Yet there's also a sense in which Jesus' death and resurrection each accomplish purposes related to salvation in their own right.

With regard to Jesus' death, I'm not sure the "Jesus died to save us from our sins" mantra is the best bumper sticker saying for trying to convey the reason for Christ's death. Don't get me wrong, as I said above, this summary is true. Yet this isn't the only lens the New Testament gives us for understanding the reason for Jesus' death. If we are going to put the rationale for Christ's death in a nutshell in talking about Jesus, is this the best nutshell?

Some might say we shouldn't even try to use a bumper sticker phrase to explain the reason for Jesus' crucifixion. They might say the implications of this earth-shaking event are nearly beyond

---

2. This understanding of the nature of sin is a continual theme in N. T. Wright's book entitled *The Day the Revolution Began.*

words and they certainly can't be reduced to a mere handful of words. Maybe that's true.

But my mind is so simple that it's helpful for me to have brief word anchors for the most important things, and there's nothing more important to grasp, to the degree we can, than why Jesus voluntarily died on the cross. These brief word anchors may not offer a full explanation, but they form a good starting point for my memory. They comprise a sound springboard designed to push me in a good direction about crucial matters.

So here's a bumper sticker saying to consider: Jesus' death shows us what love is. The go-to summary verse for many Christians in describing Jesus' ministry is John 3:16, and that's a really great verse.[3] Yet I wonder if 1 John 3:16 is better for bumper sticker purposes: "This is how we know what love is: Jesus Christ laid down his life for us" (NIV).

At the center of Jesus' death on the cross is the forgiveness of sins and the heart of forgiveness is love. Jesus said the greatest commandment—the most important thing we do—is all about love: Love God with all that you are and love your neighbor as yourself (Mark 12:28–31). Since Jesus said that the most important thing we do is all about love, then, of course, the pinnacle of his earthly ministry (i.e. his death) has to be all about love. This is confirmed in 1 John 3:16 where we're told that we know what love really is through Jesus' voluntary decision to lay down his life for us.

How does Jesus' death teach us what love is? Think of it this way: God in Christ would rather die than retaliate against his enemies.[4] At his arrest, Matthew's gospel tells us that one of Jesus' disciples took his sword and attacked a servant of the high priest. Jesus said, "Put your sword back into its place; for all who take the sword will perish by the sword. Do you think that I cannot appeal

3. "For God so loved the world that he gave his only Son, so that everyone who believes in him may not perish but may have eternal life" (John 3:16, NRSV).

4. Brian Zahnd says something similar: "In Christ we discover a God who would rather die than kill his enemies." (Zahnd, *Sinners in the Hands of a Loving God*, 87.)

to my Father, and he will at once send me more than twelve legions of angels?" (Matthew 27:52–53, NRSV).

Jesus had the power not only to stop those who were killing him but to retaliate against them. He adamantly refused to use that power. Indeed, he said this was an improper use of power that only leads to an escalating cycle of violence. Rather than wiping out his enemies, he let them kill him. More than that, he blessed those who took his life, praying that the heavenly Father would forgive then (Luke 23:34).

This is how we know what love is.

Christ, through the cross, showed us a radically different way to relate to one another. God's power is not seen in its truest sense through grand displays of might or glorious conquests as we typically understand these. God's power is most clearly revealed through Jesus' exercise of love for his enemies on the cross. It's a love that exposes true justice by allowing injustice to mete out its worst while all the while possessing the means to stop it. It's a love so committed to nonviolence that it allows violence to take its full toll while having the power to easily crush all attackers. It's a love that dies for the ungodly (Romans 5:6) rather than punishing the ungodly even when there's good reason for punishment.

Certainly one of the ways that Jesus saves us from our sinfulness is by showing us the righteous path of living. Imagine a world in which Christ's radical love becomes the norm. Is this a pipe dream? God doesn't think so. John 3:17 says, "God did not send the Son into *the world* to condemn *the world*, but in order that *the world* might be saved through him" (NRSV, emphasis mine). Jesus doesn't think so. He promised that he would draw *all people* to himself through his death (John 12:32). He prayed that the heavenly Father's will would be done on earth as it is in heaven (Matthew 6:10), and certainly he expected that prayer to be answered in the affirmative.

Jesus' love is designed not to condemn the world but to save the whole world. He believed his love displayed on the cross would be so attractive that ultimately everyone would be drawn to him and his way. He expected God's will to love to be realized on earth as it is in heaven. We know what love is through Jesus' love for his enemies revealed on the cross and he was (and is) convinced that his love will triumph. As he died he said, "It is finished" (John 19:30, NRSV), a cry of victory as he set in motion an irreversible revolution of love that, in part, saves us from our sinful ways by revealing a new and better way.

Why did Jesus die on the cross? To show us what love is. And his love is the victory that overcomes the world.

Questions to ponder

- In what ways can you envision talking with others about Jesus' death?

- In what ways might the news of the day open doors to talk about the love Jesus revealed on the cross?

- In what ways might twisted notions of love in our culture provide opportunities to talk about the way Jesus' death shows us what love really is?

Just one conversation idea among many

Friend: I was at the mall the other day and I saw two cars parked nose-to-nose in one parking space, each sticking halfway out of the parking space. The drivers of the cars were standing outside of the cars and they were fighting over that parking space! What's the world coming too?

Christian: That's crazy and it seems like the world is at least that crazy on a lot of days. Dionne Warwick was right—"What the world needs now is love . . ." We need the kind of love that Jesus showed on the cross. He let himself be killed unjustly when he had the power to stop it. Certainly he would have let someone else have a parking space rather than fighting over it. The world will be a better place as his kind of love catches on . . .

4

His Resurrection

**The big idea: Jesus' resurrection shows us there is
hope beyond the absolute worst.**

There's a detail about the risen Jesus' appearance to Thomas
that has long intrigued me (John 20:24–29). Thomas is called
"Doubting Thomas" because, after hearing the report of the other
disciples that Jesus had been raised, he said he wouldn't believe
it unless he saw and touched Jesus' scars from the crucifixion.
Thomas' nickname is a bit of a bum rap. The gospel accounts of the
resurrection reveal that all the disciples were slow to believe yet
only Thomas is dubbed a doubter.

When Thomas saw the risen Jesus a week after declaring his
doubt, the Lord invited him to touch his scars. There's no indi-
cation that Thomas actually touched the scars—seeing may have
been sufficient for him as he declared his belief in the resurrection.
But what gets me about this resurrection appearance is that Jesus
had scars to show to Thomas.

Christ was the first to receive a glorious resurrection body.
Perhaps all believers have wondered about the nature of resurrection bodies. Jesus, in his resurrection body, was able pass through
locked doors (John 20:19), yet he made a point to show the

disciples that he was not a ghost—he had flesh and bones and ate food after his resurrection (Luke 24:39–43). Still, there's much we don't know about resurrection bodies.

In whatever way Jesus' mortal body put on immortality (1 Corinthians 15:53) through the resurrection, the transformation didn't include the removal of the scars of his crucifixion. I don't know whether or not believers will have utterly perfect bodies through the resurrection, but I'm encouraged by the scars that remain on Jesus' resurrection body. Those scars are emblems of hope beyond the absolute worst thing that can happen to anyone.

Jesus died an utterly shameful and extremely painful death. Magnifying his humiliation and agony was the injustice of his execution. The perfect Son of God who deserved the highest praise and adoration was instead tortured and killed as the worst criminal. Of all the bad things to happen to humans through the centuries, the breathtaking magnitude of the injustice of Jesus' execution must rank it as the worst thing to ever happen to one person. I simply cannot conceive of something worse than the person most deserving of all the best receiving instead the absolute worst punishment known at the time.

So I consider the scars on Jesus' resurrection body to be the promise of hope beyond the absolute worst. Scars never go away completely, but neither do they hurt anymore.[1] Christ's scars remind us that he triumphed over the worst the world can dish out. The Apostle Paul called Christ's resurrection the first fruits—the promise—of the coming resurrection of the faithful (1 Corinthians 15:20). Jesus' resurrection offers hope beyond the grief, the injustice, the pain that we endure along our journey of faith, not to mention fundamentally transforming the world for the better.

Hope is a nearly universally beloved word in our culture and it's also nearly universally misunderstood. At least the word hope is misunderstood in terms of the New Testament notion of the concept. "Hope" in our society can refer to a wish that is unlikely to be fulfilled like someone holding a lottery ticket who says, "I hope I win the jackpot!"

1. Yancey, *The Jesus I Never Knew*, 219.

In contrast, the Greek word normally translated "hope" means "confident anticipation." Hope in the New Testament is about something great that's around the corner that's anticipated confidently. We truly believe it's going to happen, we're just not sure when. Jesus' resurrection means that his followers can confidently anticipate something glorious even beyond the worst things that can possibly happen.

Christ's resurrection is the promise that his followers need not fear any longer the thing we humans tend to fear most: death. That alone is a great reason to follow him and offer him the highest praise. Yet Jesus' resurrection is about a hope bigger than the pledge of heavenly life after death, as great as that is.

Jesus' resurrection vindicates the way of life he taught and lived. His birth shows us that lowliness is next to godliness. His life shows us that God insists on treating us much better than we deserve and that God expects us to do the same toward others. His voluntary death on the cross when he possessed the power to stop it and retaliate shows us what love is. His resurrection vindicates his way as the best way—the only way of real hope.

In Paul's great exposition of the resurrection in 1 Corinthians 15, there's one word in this verse that grabs my attention: "If for this life only we have hoped in Christ, we are of all people most to be pitied" (1 Corinthians 15:19, NRSV). Notice the word "only." Our hope in Christ is not only for life in this world, praise God. But the structure of this sentence indicates that our hope in Christ is in part for life in this world.

Paul was writing possibly to correct an erroneous teaching among a group of Christians that there is no resurrection of the dead and that hoping in Christ is *all about* life in this world. He was saying there's more to it—a lot more. Many Christians of our culture seem to embrace a nearly opposite extreme to the one that worried Paul in thinking that hope in Christ has very little to do with this world and it's almost entirely about looking forward to the next world.

After his resurrection, the emphasis of Jesus' message to his followers wasn't, "Don't worry, now you'll go to heaven when you die." Instead, he focused on a priority in their way of living. He clearly possessed hope in the impact his life, death, and resurrection would have upon the world.

The risen Christ instructed his followers to go and make disciples of all peoples, teaching them to obey all that he commanded (Matthew 28:18–20). He commanded them to proclaim repentance and forgiveness of sins to all peoples (Luke 24:46–48). He told them to be his witnesses all around the world (Acts 1:8). It's clear that Jesus saw his resurrection as a vindication of the way of life he modeled and taught and he expected his way to transform the world. So Jesus' resurrection shows us there is hope beyond the absolute worst not only in the sense of a heavenly hope when we die but in the sense that this world's worst can be transformed now by the life of the risen Christ as his body—the church—engages his mission.

Catastrophes regularly leave many dead or struggling to survive. Wars continue to claim many lives while creating countless desperate refugees. Many live in fear of terrorist attacks or they are left grieving in the wake of one. Besides large-scale human suffering, many face personal difficulties—physical ailments, financial problems, job stress, relational woes, the pangs of grief . . . The list is endless. Thanks to Jesus, there's hope. We can confidently anticipate glorious things beyond the absolute worst both now and forever.

Questions to ponder

- In what specific ways can the resurrection of Christ be used to address hopelessness?

- How might the hope the resurrection of Christ offers beyond this existence be used to talk about Jesus?

- How might the hope the resurrection of Christ offers for life now be used to talk about Jesus?

Just one conversation idea among many:

Friend: [In a restaurant where a news broadcast is on TV.] Good grief, the world is going to hell in a handbasket. Things are getting worse and worse.

Christian: Yeah, I used to think that way too. But my outlook has changed. I think Jesus has big plans for the world—great plans. His resurrection vindicates his way of life and it shows me that, through living according to his way, there's hope beyond the absolute worst in this world . . .

5

His ongoing Presence

The big idea: The coming of the Holy Spirit shows us that Jesus is with us always.

In February of 2013 a couple known only as John and Mary walked a trail on their property in Northern California as they had done nearly every day for many years. On this particular day they saw the edge of an old can sticking out of the ground along the trail. They dug it up and discovered that it was full of gold coins. After further investigation, with the aid of a metal detector, they found seven more cans containing gold coins.

It's known as the Saddle Ridge Hoard. The 1,427 coins dated from 1847 to 1894 have been valued at over $10 million dollars. The cache, the largest collection of buried gold ever found in the United States, includes 14 of the finest coin specimens of their type ever discovered. One particularly rare coin is valued at $1 million.[1]

John and Mary literally walked over pots of gold on their property daily for years. For a long time they lived as if a treasure in their midst didn't exist. Many followers of Christ do much the same every day.

---

1. Williams, "Who Buried the $10 Million in Coins."

After his resurrection and just before his ascension back to the heavenly Father, Jesus promised his followers that he would be with them always (Matthew 28:20). That promise was realized a few days after Christ's ascension on the day of Pentecost when all believers were "filled with the Holy Spirit" (Acts 2:4, NRSV). Perhaps the most important thing to remember about the Holy Spirit is that the Spirit is the real presence of God. The Spirit isn't some substitute for God until we get the real thing. The Holy Spirit is truly God with us, God in us, now.

Since this study is about the story of Christ, it's important to note the intertwining of Jesus and the Spirit. This isn't the place to get into a full-fledged discussion of the Trinity. Yet in the mystery of the uniqueness and the unity in the Persons of the Trinity, the New Testament points to the union of Christ and the Spirit. In numerous places the Holy Spirit is called the "Spirit of Jesus" or "the Spirit of Christ" (e.g. Acts 16:7; Romans 8:9; Philippians 1:19; 1 Peter 1:11). In 2 Corinthians 3:17, we read that "the Lord is the Spirit" (NRSV). In the very next verse we see that our ongoing transformation into the image of Christ "comes from the Lord, who is the Spirit" (2 Corinthians 3:18, NIV).

The Holy Spirit indwells all followers of Christ and the Lord is the Spirit. Jesus is with us always.

On the heels of saying the Lord is with us because the Spirit is with us, the Apostle Paul asserts that "we have this treasure in clay jars" (2 Corinthians 4:7, NRSV). The mind-boggling reality is that in the frail "clay" bodies of Christ-followers is the greatest treasure that exists—a treasure infinitely greater than a mere $10 million worth of gold coins. Yet, like John and Mary did for years, many Christians overlook the treasure that is the Spirit of Christ that they already possess—or perhaps this treasure possesses them.

We may get a better handle on the inestimable value of the treasure that is the Spirit of Christ when we consider the purpose of the Holy Spirit in the lives of believers. The Spirit is the deposit, guaranteeing a glorious inheritance (Ephesians 1:13–14). Yet, while the Spirit of Christ is the deposit or promise of the glorious future of believers, the ministry of the Holy Spirit is largely about our lives now.

Already I've mentioned the role of the Spirit in transforming us more into Christ's likeness with ever-increasing glory (2 Corinthians 3:17–18). This alone reveals the unsurpassed value of the treasure that is the Spirit. It's astounding that this real presence in the lives of Christ-followers is constantly shaping us into the glorious likeness of the Savior of the world. Yet there's much more.

Paul wrote about the Spirit of Jesus helping him in difficult circumstances (Philippians 1:19) and he promised believers that the Spirit would help us in our weakness (Romans 8:26). The Spirit produces in the lives of believers the glorious fruits of love, joy, peace, patience, kindness, generosity, faithfulness, gentleness, and self-control (Galatians 5:22–23). The love of God is poured into the hearts of believers through the Spirit (Romans 5:5).

Before his death, Jesus comforted his followers with the promise of the Holy Spirit. He said that he would not leave them orphaned, but the Spirit would come as a teacher and their advocate when Jesus was gone physically (John 14:18–25). He assured them that the Holy Spirit would be their guide in life, showing them the way of truth and glorifying him (John 16:13–14).

The Spirit of Christ fills believers for the purpose of engaging us in the most important, the most meaningful work in the world. In Acts 1:8, right before his ascension, Jesus promised his followers that the Spirit would empower them to be his witnesses everywhere. In Peter's sermon when the Spirit came in Acts 2, he pointed to Old Testament prophesy that links the coming of the Spirit to the proclamation of God's message even as believers were proclaiming God's message through the Spirit in that moment. Furthermore, believers are provided with the resources to carry out this work in the form of spiritual gifts, each a "manifestation of the Spirit" (1 Corinthians 12:7, NRSV). Jesus is with us through the Spirit, empowering us to be his witnesses and to declare his message, and he grants us gifts of the Spirit for this, the greatest, most significant work in the world.

I could go on with other New Testament images of the work of the Spirit in the lives of believers. Yet this short list should be sufficient to help us to see that, not only are believers not alone, believers are not alone in the most glorious sense imaginable. Christ is with us, in us, and for us always. And if Christ is with us, in us, and for us, who can stand against us in any way that really counts for time and eternity?

In my experience, the ongoing presence of Jesus through the Spirit is never mentioned as a part of Jesus' story that should be used in witnessing encounters. I wonder if we are missing an opportunity by not talking about the Spirit of Christ when we talk about Jesus. In Acts 2, when the Holy Spirit came at Pentecost, unbelieving onlookers were amazed at what the Spirit was doing through believers and asked, "What does this mean?" (Acts 2:12, NRSV). Peter got the floor and explained that the deeds they witnessed were the work of the Spirit in the followers of Christ and he proceeded to talk about Jesus and about 3,000 people were saved.

Maybe we should learn something from this pivotal moment from Christian history. Curiosity about the work of the Spirit of Christ in believers opened the door to talk about Jesus and thousands were saved. Could it be that as we allow the Spirit of Christ in us to work through us the curiosity of others will be aroused and doors will be opened to talk about Jesus?

Questions to ponder

- How might we nurture a deeper awareness to the value of the treasure that is Jesus' ongoing presence in order to use this part of Jesus' story in witnessing opportunities?

- In what ways might you discuss with others the reality and the wonder of Christ's presence working through you?

- In what ways can you envision using the promise of Jesus' abiding presence in addressing the loneliness that some experience?

Just one conversation idea among many

Friend: [After a potentially explosive situation.] Wow! I don't know how you kept your cool. I would have gone off on him and I would have gotten into serious trouble. How did you keep from blowing a gasket?

Christian: Well, I'd like to think it's Jesus in me. The New Testament says that Jesus is with Christians always through his Spirit, strengthening us and guiding us. That's not to say I'm perfect by any stretch of the imagination—far from it! But I believe there's a real Presence in my life influencing me toward a better way to live . . .

6

His Return

The big idea: Jesus will return to earth at an unexpected time, so we must always be ready.

I Googled what I could remember of a book title to make sure I got it right for this chapter and I was surprised to discover that this particular book is still available, at least in a digital format. The book is entitled *88 Reasons Why the Rapture Will Be in 1988* and it was written by Edgar Whisenant. In case you don't know, "the Rapture" is a reference to the second coming of Christ. You can probably see why I was surprised this book is still available. Whisenant, a former NASA engineer who died in 2001, predicted that Jesus would return and rapture the church between September 11 and 13 in 1988.[1]

Even though his prediction of Christ's return failed, as of this writing, the book outlining Whisenant's rationale is still available for purchase. Amazon shoppers are using reviews of the book to scoff at it and to make serious statements about the way it impacted them. One reviewer said the book frightened him/her as a child and he/she attributes his/her generalized anxiety disorder in part to the trauma it caused. A reviewer named Jason says *88 Reasons*

---

1. Hirsley, "Read Fast."

was the catalyst that caused him and his wife to reconsider their Christian faith and to ultimately become atheists.[2]

Of course, Whisenant's prediction was not the first of its kind nor has it been the last—there have been many. Whisenant himself went on to predict numerous other dates for the return of Christ. As I write, a prediction of the rapture that made headlines failed a few weeks ago and the author has revised his date by about six months.[3]

Efforts to predict the return of Christ are just wrong. Jesus said so. In Acts 1, a few days after Jesus' resurrection and just before his ascension, the apostles asked him if he was going to restore the kingdom to Israel right then. In other words, they wanted to know if Jesus was going to bring about the culmination of things in that moment. In response, Jesus said, "It is not for you to know the times or periods that the Father has set by his own authority" (Acts 1:7, NRSV). Christ said the timing of the culmination of all things is *not for his followers to know.*

Jesus also said his return will be unexpected: "Therefore you also must be ready, for the Son of Man is coming at an unexpected hour" (Matthew 24:44, NRSV). Since Christ promised that the timing of his return will be a surprise, his followers shouldn't be in the business of trying to predict the timing. For one thing, followers of Christ shouldn't be attempting to make him wrong about the unexpected nature of his return. For another thing, Jesus isn't going to be wrong about his return being a surprise, so it's fruitless to try to take the surprise out of it by attempting a prediction. Jesus said his return will be unexpected and we can count on him being right.

Because Christ's return will be unexpected, he urged his followers to remain in a perpetual state of readiness, which makes sense. Jesus used the illustration of our preparations for a thief

2. Reviews of *88 Reasons Why the Rapture Will Be in 1988* viewed at https://www.amazon.com/Reasons-Rapture-Will-1988-Rosh-Hash-Ana-ebook/dp/B01BE1L88G/ref=cm_cr_arp_d_pl_foot_top?ie=UTF8#customerReviews on October 5, 2017.

3. Greshko, "No, The World Will Not End"

(Matthew 24:43–44). If we knew when a thief was coming, then we would be there with law enforcement on hand to stop the break in. But we don't know when thieves are coming, so we try to stay ready for them with locks, motion lights, and perhaps an alarm system. In like manner, we must stay ready for the return of Christ.

What does preparedness for the return of Christ look like? In the context of urging readiness for his return, Jesus said, "Blessed is that slave whom his master will find at work when he arrives" (Matthew 24:46, NRSV). As discussed previously, the risen Christ gave his followers work to do: Making disciples and teaching them to obey his commands, proclaiming his message of forgiveness, being his witnesses, etc. His basic call to his disciples is, "Follow me." We are to strive always to faithfully follow his teaching and his example. We ready ourselves for Christ's return by going about the work to which he calls us, seeking to follow him faithfully.

Reading the tea leaves in the news for evidence that Christ is coming soon is a popular, useless exercise. Jesus told his followers to expect him to come soon (Revelation 22:20). I know, it has been a long time. Yet this doesn't change the fact that New Testament writers indicate that we should expect Jesus to return soon. This being the case, there's no need whatsoever to look at news events or astrological phenomena or anything else to make the determination that Jesus is coming soon. We must live as though Christ may return at any moment.

Christ's return will be visible to everyone. We read in Revelation 1:7 that he will come with the clouds and "every eye will see him" (NRSV). While Jesus' first advent to earth was in humility, his exalted status will be evident at his return. He told his followers that he will return "with power and great glory" (Matthew 24:30, NRSV).

Many believe earth will be destroyed at Jesus' return and believers will be whisked away to a separate place known as heaven. This isn't necessarily so. In 1 Thessalonians 4:13–18, we're told the resurrected and living believers will meet Jesus in the air at his return. Many see evidence in this passage indicating he'll then complete his descent bringing all believers with him to a renewed earth. God created the earth and declared it "very good" (Genesis 1:31, NRSV). To say that humans, with the help of the devil, mar God's very good creation to the point that it must be destroyed underestimates God's power. After all, the Apostle Paul wrote that creation waits in eager anticipation for the culmination of things and that it will be set free from its bondage (Romans 8:19–20). Believers should be prepared for the possibility that a renewed earth may be part of what we commonly refer to as heaven.

The tendency of many preachers is to use the promise of the imminent return of Christ to scare people into believing. This is not the approach of New Testament writers. Every reference to the return of Christ in the New Testament includes an ethical dimension for the followers of Christ. In other words, New Testament writers uniformly use the second coming to inspire Christ-followers to faithfulness (e.g. Colossians 3:4–5, 2 Corinthians 5:9–11, 2 Timothy 4:1–2, etc.).

The hope of Christians is ultimately bound in the promise that Jesus will return and set all things aright forever. Every tear will be wiped away and death, mourning, and pain will be no more in the reality of the new heavens and the new earth revealed when Jesus comes back (Revelation 21:1–4). May this hope inspire our faithfulness now. Besides that, since we believe Jesus is coming unexpectedly and soon, always be ready by doing the work to which he empowered us and called us through the Spirit.

Questions to ponder

- In what ways might you use the latest misguided prediction of the timing of Christ's return to talk about Jesus?

- How might you use the unexpected nature of Christ's return as an opportunity to talk about Jesus?

- How might you use your hopefulness of the return of Christ to talk about Jesus?

Just one conversation idea among many

Friend: I saw in the news that some guy has predicted that Jesus will return on the first of next month and whisk his followers away to heaven. So have you got your bags packed and ready to go?

Christian: [Laughs.] I saw that and it's ridiculous. Jesus said that his return will be unexpected—no one knows the timing. It could be today, tomorrow, next year, or a hundred years from now. But I believe he's coming back soon and that his return will be a surprise to everyone. Because of that, I try to keep my bags packed, if you know what I mean. I try to stay ready by being as faithful as I can be to his revolution of love and grace . . .

Epilogue

I hope your efforts to increase your comfort level in talking about Jesus won't end with reading this booklet. Develop a discipline of reading the New Testament regularly. Read other books about Jesus. That said, for this particular resource to benefit you the most, your use of it shouldn't stop here.

In the short chapters above I have briefly fleshed out a set a big ideas connected to Jesus' birth, life, death, resurrection, ongoing presence, and return. I warned you at the beginning that the ideas set forth here are not meant to exhaust "the boundless riches of Christ" (Ephesians 3:8, NRSV). Eternity will be insufficient to exhaust his riches. My feeble efforts are simply designed to increase our confidence in talking to others about Jesus by giving us a framework for conversations about him encapsulated in these big ideas:

- *Jesus' birth shows us that lowliness is next to godliness.*
- *Jesus' life shows us that God insists on treating us much better than we deserve and that God expects us to do the same toward others.*
- *Jesus' death shows us what love is.*
- *Jesus' resurrection shows us there is hope beyond the absolute worst.*
- *The coming of the Holy Spirit shows us that Jesus is with us always.*

- *Jesus will return to earth at an unexpected time, so we must always be ready.*

If this framework is to be helpful as an aid in the joyful, meaningful task of talking about Jesus then we need to be somewhat familiar with these big ideas on an ongoing basis. In that vein, I set out to keep this booklet short in the bold hope that it might re-read regularly. I'll even suggest a schedule. Consider reading one chapter per day on the second week of the second month of each quarter. Put it on your calendar.

I timed my re-reading of the longest chapter in this booklet (the chapter on Jesus' death). It took me a little over six minutes. Can we afford to take six minutes per day on one set week each quarter in an effort to continue to build our confidence in talking to others about Jesus?

Certainly I don't mean to suggest that this booklet is the be-all-and-end-all resource for increasing your comfort level in talking about Jesus. Again, I urge you to read the New Testament and other books on Jesus regularly. But I made this booklet short in the hope that it might be easily re-read regularly so that these big ideas might become second nature and, therefore, readily available on our minds and hearts. Our familiarity with these big ideas can help us to more easily see when doors open to talk about Jesus and increase our confidence in stepping through those open doors.

You're ready to talk about Jesus. You were ready before you read this booklet. In Mark 13:9–11, Jesus promised his followers that, as they bear testimony to him, the Holy Spirit will give them the words to say even in the most intimidating circumstances. Believe him!

Yet Jesus is far too wonderful for us to stop getting to know him more and more. And the more we get to know him, the more confident we will be in talking about him. Thanks for taking the time to get to know Christ more through this booklet. Keep on getting to know him more and keep on talking about him!

Selected Bibliography

Cohick, Lynn H. *Women in the World of the Earliest Christians: Illuminating Ancient Ways of Life*. Ada, Missouri: Baker Academic. 2009.

Greshko, Michael. *"No, the World Will Not End on April 23"* National Geographic (April 13, 2018). https://news.nationalgeographic.com/2018/04/april-23-apocalypse-nibiru-rapture-end-time-myth-science/.

Hirsley, Michael. *"Read Fast, It May be the End."* Chicago Tribune (September 1, 1989). https://www.chicagotribune.com/news/ct-xpm-1989–09–01–8901090528-story.html.

Williams, A. R. *"Who Buried the $10 Million in Coins Found by a California Couple—and Why?"* National Geographic (February 27, 2014). http://news.nationalgeographic.com/news/2014/02/140226-gold-coins-hoard-california-discovery-numismatics/.

Wright, N.T. *The Day the Revolution Began: Reconsidering the Meaning of Jesus' Crucifixion*. San Francisco: HarperOne, 2016.

Yancey, Philip. *The Jesus I Never Knew*. Grand Rapids, Michigan: Zondervan. 1995. 219.

———. *What's So Amazing About Grace?* Grand Rapids, Michigan: Zondervan. 1997.

Zahnd, Brian. *Sinners in the Hands of a Loving God: The Scandalous Truth of the Very Good news*. New York: WaterBrook, 2017.

9 781532 675393